Lyrical Seduction

Poetry with Passion

DW JONES

Order this book online at www.trafford.com
or email orders@trafford.com

Most Trafford titles are also available at major online book retailers.

Printed in the United States of America.

ISBN: 978-1-4669-7474-6 (sc)
ISBN: 978-1-4669-7473-9 (e)

Trafford rev. 01/14/2013

www.trafford.com

North America & international
toll-free: 1 888 232 4444 (USA & Canada)
phone: 250 383 6864 ✦ fax: 812 355 4082

Contents

AIR

Body Oils,

candle lit room-

Love making at its finest.

The scents

OH how they mingle.

ADDICTION

I inhale your perfume, your essence,
and the smell of your hair.
My eyes are dilated and glazed,
Clouds roll away and the Sun shines forever.

I taste your lips,
and sate my hunger with your flesh.
Babylon falls and all is well.

You course through my veins,
Causing rational thought to become
confused, crowded, and chaotic.
Your love incapacitates my mind.

Now I tremble as I crave your presence.
Disordered thought gives way to emptiness.
My mind feels as if its wasted, yet fixed on you.
My body sweats, yearning denied pleasures.
My heart beats like thunder, as it withdraws
to the safety of the darkness.

You're like a powerful opiate
I want,
I need,
I have to have my fix.

Ascension

People are too grounded,
feet holding fast to the security Mother Earth offers
but this safety and assurance
keeps us from flying with the Angels.

All of nature reaches for the sun.
The leaves on the trees forever yearn to reach higher,
embracing its warmth.
Flowers follow its majestic rays daily in
soon praise.

Birds soar
Rising on warm currents,
butterflies flutter by,
while bees and seeds
gently kiss the breeze

all return to gravity
but for time they all touch heaven
release your fear and be lifted.

Beautiful

White and pure as the
finest alabaster
or Black as volcanic ash
source of nurturing Earth

Yellow as Our Sun
that brings us warmth and light
or Red as Clay with its with
its healing ways

Brown as soil which grows all that
sustain us
we are varied as the Planet on which
we live

Aside from the ignorance that might
sway to the opposite pole
We are all Beautiful

God has given this
to protect our physical,
The garment of our Spirit and Soul
this thing we're in
is only Skin

Between Worlds

Pulled from head and heals
Heart and Spirit
I am torn by forces intangible
But real, and strong.

Weightless in this emptiness
The gravity of distant worlds rend my being
My satisfaction knows not its origin
My torment knows not its end

Feelings so minute, defying description,
they exist in the very fiber of me.
Feelings so immense, no words can suffice,
dwarfing the span of the heavens.

Love, Lust, Loyalty and Trust
offer no solution as
I struggle with decisions
more difficult than right and wrong.

Every choice, sacrifice
Every decision, bittersweet
No direction to turn
that will leave me unscarred.

One, between worlds
cannot be divided,
I will be strong.
I will not regret.

DWJones072011

BREATH

I wake and breathe a prayer,
rejoicing that a small piece of heaven
can trace my lungs.

Through Stress and Frustration
My breath gives me a moment.
A second to admire the beauty of
an orchid.

They remind me of you.

A breath in trade
for a moment in time.
A second, to smell their scent

Your essence

One day my eyes will not open,
My heart will not beat or Love,
My life will not live
And in my last breath,
a prayer for you.

CAPTIVE

Your silence speaks
in deafening tones
as your eyes command
my soul to submit.
Stronger than any Shaman's spell,
your mouth whispers
enchanting incantations.
Sounds bounding,
resounding in my ear
like a sirens song,
summoning my essence to you.

Being a prisoner of your passion
My needs are met "By the look in your eyes
and the sincerity of your words."
My darkness is pierced by
Your love's light,
Life is reborn,
And I don't want to be free.

Committed. Only the insane
should be committed.
Devotion, the bars of my captivity.
Love, inescapable walls.
Your passion has me enslaved.
Yet your tenderness sets my mind free?
Maybe I am certifiably insane—

I want a solitary window in my room.
One view of the world in which
you reside.

Watching you safe in his arms—
Jealous of myself.

DWJones Feb'99

Change

In the macrocosm of things
we are infinitesimally small.
I am even less than nothing,
Yet I hope the waves created by
the things and people I touch
Positively Change The World.

Conclusion

It's been a while now,
And I can't wait for passion to
rise and fall and rise again;
as the ocean's waves.
With you in mind, I feel what I need,
but distance that powerful foe to overcome,
keeps me at bay.
I long to taste your secrets,
wet and sweet.
Experience your touch,
Feel the moisture of your lips.
I long to suckle your breast,
Nourishment for an unsated fantasy.
I long to cover you in oils by candle-light,
Scented and warm like your skin.
Your body, magnificent creation,
Soft and firm, moist, never dry,
An inferno, like the sun in Imperial Glory . . .

. . . yet inviting like a cool moon-lit night.
with you lying next to me, on top of me, &
under me,
I fear NOTHING,
except our CONCLUSION.

Crucified

God is Love,
And the Love he teaches
like a mantle I bestowed to you.

But like His own,
you received me not.
You took the Love I gave and mocked.

A spear to the center of my heart
revealed the tears I cried, as I lay
on the cross of your betrayal,
Crucified.

Déjà Vu

I knew you once before
Now you look at me with a stranger's eyes.
Images flash,
memories of a love that could never die.
Boundaries of time bended, transcended
By something greater than devotion
Guinevere to Arthur's time
Cleopatra to Anthony's side

Why does this new birth incarnate poison me so?
Why will you not caress my ear with the words
of your soul, transplanted there by your tender lips.

I know you, of this I'm sure.
But your scorning gaze betrays my heart.
Staring as if I were a leprous demon,
spewed from the rotting quim of Hades

What was my past transgression?
What was my crime?
Do you not see past this form reborn?
As I see my angel true.
What HELL is this?
What cruel Déjà Vu.

DWJones
032011

echoes

Bodies entwine,

Rapture.

As time passes,
only echoes remain
of our PASSION.
PASSION.
PASSION.
PASSION.

Essence

New lovers can't compare to the familiar essence of
your skin,
that fragrant aroma I know.
Your touch sends shivers up and down my spine;
like a cool pleasant November wind, bringing the first
flakes of snow.

It's not unlike the feeling of seeing a
child's first Christmas Day,
or feeling the first warm rain of May that
whets my appetite for long nights with you.

From deep within,
a craving for that familiar essence of your skin.

Forgotten

You've prayed for what seems a lifetime,
Yearning for your ship to come in.
Then one day unexpectedly,
while the tide was high,
slowly it docked in your harbor.
First, you think it's some cruel apparition
haunting you from your dreams,
a cruel joke of your mind,
but you touched it felt it,
knew it was real,
yours to have, yet you did not board.

It waited with a patient diligence that you seemed
to ignore
Caught in your own perpetual madness

The horn sounded, and your vessel set sail
and now you wonder . . .

Thunder rolls from a distant storm
As God says,
"You have forgotten what you have prayed for."

The horizon becomes empty and the sun sets,
Familiar clouds rage in on torrid winds,
and the rain falls cold.

FRIENDS

The first time I touched you, I knew it from then;
It was told to me by the perfect softness of your skin.
Years of anticipation boiling within,
A pressure released by the perfect softness
of your skin.
Seeing you for the first time once again, embracing you,
and the perfect softness of your skin.

As I gazed into your eyes there was an
unexpected reaction;
A satisfaction.
My soul rested easy on the bosom of what
I hoped to be.
You leaned in close to me.
I breathed your breath and prepared to set my heart
free.
Holding you close, I caught your scent,
A baby soft essence, Innocence.

Closer you leaned in,
As my hand caressed the perfect softness of your skin,
You, kissed my cheek and called me . . .
Friend.

Garden

Does he buy you flowers, lovely tokens of his affection?
Did you ever stop to think on these representations of
his love to you?
Roses, Lilies, Daisies and Irises all dead, cut from the
heart of their existence. Each green leaf, each pastel
petal struggling to open, a deception.
They offer no growth, no seed, no life, no future.
For less time than a few breaths you fawn over these
icons of what you wish to be, then as the quickened
beat of your heart slows, they wilt away.
When will you see the like again, a birthday,
an anniversary, an apology.
You find pleasure in what he bestows.
Dare you open your eyes to see the truth?
He offers you that of everyone else;
And my garden, growing, flowering, bearing fruit, is
empty?

GENESIS

This World Is Lost,
As are those who seek happiness in it.
Life teaches its lessons with blatant disregard,
And like disobedient children we refuse
to Look, Listen and Learn.
We open doors and welcome Armageddon.
Wars, Tribulations, Chaos, enter Abaddon

As a final darkness falls and Brimstone heats the air
I feel you breathing,
Deep purposeful gasp
Becoming quick and shallow.
You look at me and smile;

I see a new Beginning and I'm unafraid.

Handle This

So you're an insatiable creature
with an appetite that won't quit.
Lay back then love and take in
this Dic-taction, stimulation, quelling
all frustration. Filling you with
insatiable emotion, Primal Heat
in virgin gestation.

This, just the beginning for the
emotions your feeling.
I'll kiss you from lips to fingertips
and back again
until you hit the ceiling.

Passions screaming, an inferno burning,
as you whisper my name.
You marvel silently
while your essence came.

Caressing your body and stroking your hips,
until you're sated, my love will ne'er quit.
I'll bestow a world of pleasure that will never
wane.
Unless you drive me . . . . I'll drive you insane.

So you're an insatiable creature
with an appetite that never quits.
Tell me then love, Can you handle this?

Have you ever made love with all your senses

Have you ever made love
with all your senses?
Embrace with your soul—
the pleasure of total fulfillment
even before your pelvic muscle tenses.

It starts with your state of mind,
here as you read between these sultry lines,
Contemplating the disappointing possibility
of creating memories
that will outshine a future reality

Tell me with your eyes
the allure you feel as slowly you disrobe,
freeing your physical form
of these chains called clothes.
Slowly led to a bath of rose petals and milk,
shortly thereafter a bed of pillowed silk.
From head to toe anointed with scented oils
As candles glint unsteady flames
Your blood begins a measured boil.

Soft kisses to the neck
manifest lustful desires
Touching softly, stroking attentively,
biting carefully,

You seek to possess and enslave me
in your passion.
Craving inches of pressure pushing
against the inner reaches of your Spirit,
you conceive a Rhythmic pounding
timed with the beat of your heart.

As fragrant flavors fill the air
from oils and candles alike,
our scents too mingle—
a wet sweaty night tearing apart
our souls with sinful indulgences.

I know your desires,
You yearn for me know your body
like I know my own
That spot just above you hip that tickles,
but makes you moan.
You want me to know your curves,
hands navigating with no restriction
creating circles of pressure,
pleasure, and pain
your mortal perception not understanding
where one ends, or one begins.
Confusion, Contradiction.

Fingernails to your side
and lower back.
A clandestine attack—
Delusion as I kiss you softly,
your ankles and the area behind your knee
and a finger pressed against "That Spot"
that makes you want to pee.
I can hear your sighs,
deep breathing be-com-ing shal-low
as you whisper "in me".
You hunger for all that makes
your sweet nectar flow
Longing to be caressed
by a velveteen tongue,
slow—
down below.

Ecstasy in a friendship that transcends boundaries of
what a friendship should be
I know what you want,
I saw it in your eyes the day we met.
You yearn for the freedom of your innermost soul
trapped by the veil of this worldly existence.
A freedom only experienced when you
let goof all you have, and all you are,
and release—<breath out loud>—in orgasmic passion.

Here you lay—
exhausted on this silken bed—
and I have only bathed your body in milk,
and your mind in thoughts of rapture.
You lost yourself in these formless verses
and that candle's glimmering—

I have only just begun my massage,
But you have gone ahead without me.

DWJones060122011

Labels

Black Artist
Spanish Writer
Chinese Actor
Why do we use Labels?

George Washington was not called
Our first White President
but Barak Obama is Labeled
Our First Black President
Sotomayor
First Latina Supreme Court Judge
Sidney Poitier
First African American to win an Academy Award
The List goes on, however
None are labeled White, Caucasian, European

If we were considered equal from the start
we would not need the additional recognition
If we are equal now, Why are We Still Labeled?

I AM a writer
A singer
A poet
A doctor
A lawyer
A Man
A Woman
I am just like you
I do what I do with skill and passion
I succeed and fail as all others do

I am Human,
God's child;
And I need no other Labels
Except, whether right or wrong,
those I Choose for Myself.

DWJones 012011

Letting Go

I sit, head hanging,
face to palms in the
brilliant bleakness of the night.

A single beam of moonlight
my only defender from the nothing
of all else around.

My head rises and I stare deeply
At the lines on my hands pondering
How you have gone from me.

The lines on my hands . . .
. . . I know them well.

DWJones
092004

Life's Manuscript

Each of us writes our
own book of life.

Though many a hand
may contribute an editorial;
its composing, editing and publication,
is ultimately in our hands.

DWJones
042011

LOOKING BACK

Remember the fourth grade,
When just a kiss would thrill you to your toes.
It was all so simply exhilarating,
Before it was about sex, marriage and tomorrow.

Remember the bleachers, the stairs, sunlit fields
and stormy nights;
Remember the champagne, slow music,
silk sheets and candlelight.

Remember when you lived for today—
Remember when you enjoyed Love—
Remember those older told you it wasn't what you felt.
Puppy love they called it with all their wisdom.

Well I'm older and wiser
And life's complications made me forget too,
But what I wouldn't give to walk again
In that young person's shoes

Lost

I love being lost—
The feeling of not knowing
what's coming next.
What's just around the corner;
Left, Right Forward and Back
All appear different yet maintain
a similar unfamiliarity.
Beads of sweat trickle, apprehension,
heart pounding anxiety.

I love being lost—
A good book;
word to line, author controlling,
scene to chapter, plot unfolding.
Building consistent pressure focused
toward a heightened climaxing.

I love being lost—
In my writing *a freedom*
from all Earthly worries.
Freedom to hold hostage those who
will glimpse into My World
with chains of their own imagination,
fantasies, and desires.
An uneasy but certain pleasure.

Most of all
I love being lost behind the big brown rivers of your eyes,
In the warm boundless reaches of your soul.
In You I'm Lost.

Gryphon
12/24/04
READ BOLD PRINT
FOR A SEPARATE TREAT
IN THE FIRST

MASTURBATION

Have you masturbated today?
Touched the walls of your intellect
Expanding your proportions with tools,
the girth of which stretch you
leaving you satisfied but longing.

Have you masturbated?
Titillated and stimulated your imagination
Inspiring the erection of perpetually flaccid fantasies
considerably beyond commonplace thought.

Have you masturbated today?
Whetting your desire
For more intense indulgence of primal urges,
Not sated by the mundane repetition
of rutted life.

Have you masturbated?
Awakened your senses to awareness,
Knowledge, and Overstanding.

Masturbate to an art:
In spoken word,
or illustration,
or sound,
Masturbate to
all the wonders of the world around.
And your climax will intensify.

N-SATIABLE

A kiss, sensual
as a beam of moonlight
licking the ocean's naked wetness.
Beneath a cloudless sky
the darkness cannot hide this affair.

Passions rise as hands and fingers
caress and see what other senses long
to experience.
Hips, like mountains, border a valley
carved by the richest flow of honey.
digits encircle flesh as the temperature
seems to rise.

Fire, flames in the blood, the heat of passion
makes clothes melt away; and only stars see
what eyes have been eager for; their twinkles
giggles of pleasure.
Sweat covered mouths ablaze, Quest for the food
of the gods—ambrosia—that sweet nectar.
Her rose bud is found, and she burst into full bloom.
Her tongue encompasses,
He exhales, skin-flames—a cold burning.

The night becomes as day as purple waves meet
a crimson sky.
Yet the stars still light the escapade, the moon
refusing to yield to the glow of day.

Insatiable cries call forth the Union
Greedy nibbles give way to a deeper yearning.
Flesh meets flesh setting spirits free to soar.

An accepted intruder into the sacred temple.
No alms given, yet all offerings received.
The choir exalts praises.
Pressure builds—Strains of pressure
Anguish and pleasure.
The Earth trembles
The sun rises
and
Her kiss invites him back again.

Virtues

(Nil Sine Magno Labore)

Where are our virtues?
Values bestowed by our parents and theirs before.
The knowledge and power of obedience,
chivalry, truth honor and responsibility.

Where are our virtues?
Stolen.
Stolen by well meaning providers, OVER-providing.
Generation following generation
Giving their progeny more, so they won't want
Inadvertently stealing what they need.
Multitudes denied the struggle that built Character,
Manhood and Womanhood.

We fail to have them wait
They fail to learn patience.
We fail to let them get tired
They become lazy and fail to be strong.
We fail to be stern
And so they fail to learn discipline.

We impart wisdom
Without allowing them to gather their own
Replacing virtues with entitlement
A generation feeling that to struggle is damaging
And to "have" for naught is life.

For all our love, we have failed
And a generation is lost
For we fail to realize without struggle
There is no progress.

Oasis

I crawl through a sea of emptiness
In the distance, an abundance of nothing.
Waves of your passion scorch my body
The heat thereof muddling the core of my mind.

My lips, desiccated, seek to be quenched by your kiss.
As beads of molten lava flow from the pores on my
forehead,
they burn tracks down my face and body
and I am offered no relief.

Undaunted, I continue my quest.
Somewhere in this nothing of an existence
There lies an Oasis, a Paradise
An ocean roars
Trees grow underneath a sapphire sky
casting shadows over your naked body
as you lay in a sea of emerald tendrils
desiring me.

At the end of my seemingly purposeless quest
Your kiss sates the thirst of my lips
Your passion satisfies the yearning of my being
And your soul extinguishes the fire that burned
without . . .
But I have not been cooled,
. . . New flames have been sparked within.

Passion

In the cool darkness of a rainy night
he gazed into her eyes but no words passed his lips.
As she reached out to touch him,
he gently took her hand and lead her outside.
She hesitated, but followed still.

Heaven watched, and shed tears at their purity.
Their bodies, drenched, yet the fires of their spirits
burned ever brighter . . . hotter.
They slowly started to kiss as raindrops seemed to
touch their wanting souls.
Thunder rolled and they both trembled,
laughed, and hugged each other.
Fear could not stop this feeling.
They gazed into the darkened sky
and heavens tears kissed their lips.

She gently took his hand, led him back inside,
Removed her wet clothes, and then his.
They looked longingly at each other, laid together,
held each other and slept

PEACHES

I LOVE TO EAT PEACHES;
FLESHY AND RIPE,
MOUNDS PLUMP,
SKIN FUZZY, TICKLING MY TONGUE.

TANGY AROMA,
SWEET-TART TASTE.
JUICY, SUCCULANT
I BITE . . .
. . . SHE BITES BACK.

Promises

As their song played
He leaned over and asked
for one last dance, one last kiss.

She pause,
Uncompromisingly she said "NO!,
because you promised me forever."

Rain of Tears

I Love the rain for it hides my tears.
While standing next to you smiling,
Shrouded by heaven's baptism is my true emotion.
So I cry as the Angels cry.

Those dreary and ominous clouds;
Veiling the lack of sparkle in my eyes,
Their darkness I adore,
for they protect your soul from concern.

Thunder hides my lamentations,
and lightning cleanses my hollow Spirit.

In the Rain of Tears my heart Rejoices.

Romance

Don't Label Me!
I Am No ROMANTIC!

ROMANCE—
A sentiment that arrives and departs
with traditional days of merit;
- Your Valentine
- Your Birthday
- Your Anniversary of whatever,
Then, No More . . .

DON'T label me a ROMANTIC:
- Though I may lay your body on silk, satin
and rose petals.
- Though I may bathe you and massage
your body with Neem and Monoi oils.
I Am NO ROMANTIC!

- I may kiss away tensions and tears, ushering your mind and body toward sensual deliberations.
  - I may prep you to dine, pour you wine,
- I may light a candle, illuminating a path for your soul to follow, melting fears of yesterday, today and tomorrow

But I AM No romantic . . .

My edges are rough

My heart is not golden

My soul, shadowy and dark

I'm not well spoken

Of the tears I've kissed, may have caused a few

So I'm NOT ROMANTIC.

I'm just Loving You.

SAXOPHONE

Standing in the subway, the street, the park;
In the sun or rain he blows a captivating tune.

People pass, some indifferent,
some disgusted by his noise.
Some entranced and astounded,
dumbfounded by his mastery of the keys,
and the notes that come from this large metal object
that looks as if it should bellow
rather than entrance your soul.

Change and bills fall into his case,
He barely notices as he is enslaved by his passion;
As I am enslaved by you.

Gryphon
062005

STILL

If you could be still
you would hear your own
life's breath pass your nostrils
as your heart whispers in your ear.

You would hear the breeze
moan its pleasures and intimate secrets
as blades of grass and dandelion puffs
tickle is body

When you learn stillness
you will hear the silence of a butterfly's
fluttering wings amidst the turbulence of the day.

In this state of quiescence
new worlds unfold and are discovered
universes of enlightenment that always existed
going unnoticed,

hidden by the absence of stillness.

DWJones
052011

STRANGERS

(Your) Deep tranquil waters hide treasures
and peril alike.
Still I wade past the shallows.

(Your) Siren's songs beacon me to come,
I see my demise,
Still I follow.

What riches are worth that of my soul?

Dreams and Fantasies of you;
Holding and Touching you.
Kissing and Hugging you.
Knowing you, and maybe even Loving you.

Thoughts of bringing Pleasure to where
Pain once resided.
Thoughts of bringing Light to where
Darkness would try to hide it.
Desires of blindfolded Ecstasies,
Bodies trembling at 110 degrees,
I hunger for the gentleness of your touch,
The savor of your bittersweet secrets.

Yet thus far,
Dreams are visions that betray reality.

Dangers
lie in the sexiness of your appeal;
and essentially,
despite our attraction, we remain
Strangers.

Submission

Do you feel that? It was slight at first,
almost non-existent, An afterthought.
But it grew. A tingle, a name intruding into daily task.
A face that flashes before sleep takes me from this
realm to the next.
There too you invade, stealing dreams of others.

You penetrate my defenses with subtle skill.
Slowly, softly you caress while gazing at my soul with
gentle eyes.
I resist, but fighting you is wasted effort.

I like the way your tongue taste on mine,
sweet nectar from golden blossoms;
the way it floats effortlessly between my lips,
feels of sinful indulgences.

Your hair, your eyes your lips;
Your breast, your waist your, hips;
Your spirit, your heart, your wit;
To all of you, I submit.

SUCCESSION

Eyes meet
Breaths exchanged
Lips unite
Tongues explore
Vagina, Breast
Penis, Chest
Convulsions climax
Knees collapse
We Exhale

The Commencing

Dim the lights my dear,
For you need no sight to feel what you revere.
Like standing in warm cascading rain,
It's a feeling to be experienced once,
and over again.
A feeling you'll never want to end.

Put all cares aside
While next to you my body glides.
Knowing my love will soon fill your
mind, heart, body & soul,
You prepare each part to take me inside,
Absolute and whole.

Tenderly my arms will enfold you.
Caress and massage while they hold you.
Feel you, tease you, as I playfully fondle
Squeeze you, as I gently kiss lips with sensuous
indulgence.

I feel your breath fiery and heavy,
burning from within.
Growing and Enhanced passion with
each attentive touch.
Moisture yields to wetness,
Waves of ecstasy,
A flood of pleasure . . . .
. . . . And we've only just begun . . .

Writing

Forethought,
the catalyst that brings pen to paper;
Tip to tongue before slowly
jotting with a broken rhythm
till the right stoke is found.

Deliberations Primed,
Beat and Depth of topic ideal,
Some now choose to type;
Pounding cold mechanical keys
to bring pleasure to the naked page.
The machine serves its purpose.

I prefer to write, using fingers
to manipulate contemplation.
Ink flows smoothly as the pen glides across the page—
Sometimes edging vertically
At other moments scratching lines that scar
marring the page
Forever to be remembered—Favorably or Not

Relinquishing the burdens of this world and
tasting only the product of my current device,
I take pleasure only in the freedom of moving
word and prose to fit position;
changing position to fit the word and expression.

Topic to statements, Opening.
Sentences to paragraphs, Position.
Clauses to Declarations, Penetration
Variation, exhilaration, summit
A gentle culmination
And sometimes . . .
An Eruption of Inspiration beyond compare,
Climax—Euphoria—al niente*—close

Forethought—
The sequel is conceived.

* **al niente**—*to nothing, fade to silence*

Broken

I am broken by life's indiscriminate sculptors
Each chiseling away a part of me,
shaping this hardened form upon which
your eyes gaze.

Eroded by time,
And jaded by life's storms my being
falters in the blistering heat of life's trails;

Still I persist, refusing to only exist.
Ire to some, admired by others,

I am broken but complete.

Eric Jones
The Gryphon
7/2007

<u>Crucified</u>

God is Love,
And the Love He teaches
like a mantle I bestowed to you.

But like His own,
you received me not.
You took the Love I gave and mocked.

A spear to the center of my heart
revealed the tears I cried, as I lay
on the cross of your betrayal,
Crucified.

Gryphon
March 2004

Legacy

WE WERE KINGS, WE BECAME SLAVES,

THEN PRISONERS OF OUR OWN DEVICES

WE MUST RETURN TO WHAT WE WERE
BEFORE WE WERE KINGS

SAME

Through fences
the other side looks just a little brighter.
Even on a moonlit night where time
Flirts with a new day.

Through fences
an imagination grows and wanders.
Through greener grass it plays.

Through fences you curse your captivity,
And on the other side –
Someone peers through his fence
And curses your freedom.

Without You

A cool rainy night and the storms of your mind are calmed by
the soothing words of another

A tempest rages in my chest and the whirl winds of my mind offer
no signs of abating.

The winter of life will be all the colder without you.

*C*oming to New York by way of Barbados, DW Jones (The Gryphon) holds a Bachelor of Science Degree in Psychology as well as several Private Sector Certifications. With this he brings certain uniqueness to the "Art of Writing". Writing in a style that any and all can relate to whether you have loved, lost, hated or have just sat back on thought about "things"; the way ordinary, finite words are arranged by this author will reach out to you passionately regardless of the tone of the poem. His works have captured the eyes of fans and critics alike, but it is agreed that his words fall in a form that is rarely if ever seen and his erotic style will be sure to keep the reader engaged and entertained.

DW Jones has been previously published in anthologies such as Sunflowers and Seashells, Dreams and Curiosities, and Forever Spoken. Overwhelming positive responses have sired this short collection, composed for your pleasure and enjoyment.